"This book is superb! No longer will teens need to suffer with anxiety and be on the sidelines of life. Full of clear, effective, and engaging strategies, this workbook will show teens exactly what to do to overcome their fears and shyness and will reassure them that they are not alone. Truly, every teen struggles with these issues to varying degrees. All teenagers would benefit from reading this book."

—Tamar Chansky, PhD, author of *Freeing Your Child from Anxiety* and *Freeing Yourself from Anxiety*

"With *The Shyness and Social Anxiety Workbook for Teens*, Jennifer Shannon has hit a bull's-eye. Each page is fun, engaging, and filled with practical strategies to help teens break free from their social fears and worries. The book is certain to become an essential resource for teens, parents, and therapists. I highly recommend it."

—Michael A. Tompkins, PhD, founding partner of the San Francisco Bay Area Center for Cognitive Therapy and author of *My Anxious Mind: A Teen's Guide to Managing Anxiety and Panic*

"Teens who follow the steps described in this book can overcome shyness and social anxiety and change their life path. Shannon's recommendations are based on the latest scientific findings, and are accompanied by delightful cartoons and drawings. An outstanding contribution."

—Jacqueline B. Persons, PhD, director of the San Francisco Bay Area Center for Cognitive Therapy and clinical professor in the department of psychology at the University of California, Berkeley

"Good basic information on social anxiety as well as how to overcome it using cognitive behavioral therapy. The concise text and abundant illustrations make the book available, easy to grasp, and engaging for teens."

—Edmund J. Bourne, PhD, author of *The Anxiety and Phobia Workbook*

"This practical and straightforward book is highly recommended for any teen who worries too much about being judged by others. These tried-and-true strategies have been shown over and over to be among the most effective methods for reducing social anxiety. Every teen who struggles with shyness should read this book!"

—Martin M. Antony, PhD, ABPP, chair of the department of psychology at Ryerson University and author of *The Shyness and Social Anxiety Workbook*

the shyness & social anxiety workbook for teens

CBT and ACT skills to help you build social confidence

JENNIFER SHANNON, LMFT

ILLUSTRATIONS BY DOUG SHANNON

Instant Help Books
A Division of New Harbinger Publications, Inc.

Distributed in Canada by Raincoast Books

Copyright © 2012 by Jennifer Shannon
           New Harbinger Publications, Inc.
           5674 Shattuck Avenue
           Oakland, CA 94609
           www.newharbinger.com

Cover design by Amy Shoup

Interior design and illustrations by Doug Shannon

Acquired by Tesilya Hanauer

Library of Congress Cataloging-in-Publication Data

Shannon, Jennifer.
  The shyness and social anxiety workbook for teens : CBT and act skills to help you build social confidence / Jennifer Shannon ; illustrated by Doug Shannon ; foreword by Christine A. Padesky.
    p. cm.
  ISBN 978-1-60882-187-7 (pbk. : alk. paper) -- ISBN 978-1-60882-188-4 (pdf e-book) -- ISBN 978-1-60882-189-1 (epub)
  1. Bashfulness--Juvenile literature. 2. Social phobia--Juvenile literature. 3. Cognitive therapy for teenagers--Problems exercises, etc. 4. Acceptance and commitment therapy--Problems, exercises, etc. I. Title.
  BF575.B3S5193 2012
  155.5'18232--dc23

           2012005433

Printed in the United States of America

19   18   17

20   19   18   17   16   15   14   13   12

Contents

Foreword

When we get anxious, we often think we suffer alone. We think we are messed up and everyone else is strong and confident. This is not true. Almost everyone gets anxious about something. Some people are afraid of spiders, others worry about lots of different things, and some people get nervous when they have to give a speech or meet new people.

The good news is that we know a lot about how to overcome anxiety. A form of psychological therapy called cognitive behavioral therapy (CBT) can help most people overcome their anxiety. CBT is based on research about how emotions work and what people can do to feel better. CBT teaches people skills that help depression, anxiety, and lots of other issues. These skills take practice, but anybody can learn them.

That's where this book comes in. It tells and shows you what you can do to overcome social anxiety and shyness. If you fill in the worksheets and try the experiments recommended, this book can help you overcome your social nervousness and feel a lot better.

Some of the exercises will make you feel nervous. That is a good thing, because one thing we know about anxiety is that it gets smaller only when we approach it rather than avoid it. To make it easier for you, the authors describe small steps you can take to help you build your confidence.

Most books like this are written for adults. That is too bad, because teenagers often get even more nervous than adults do. That's why I was so happy when Jennifer Shannon told me she and her husband were writing this book for you. Jennifer is an expert CBT therapist who has helped lots of teens overcome social anxiety. And her husband is a really good artist, which you probably already noticed when you flipped through the book. Together, they make a great team to explain clearly what social anxiety is all about and how you can overcome it.

Small steps can lead you to good places when you have a map. If you feel nervous around people, this book is your map. Take it a step at a time, and by next year you will be easily doing things that scare you this year. Think of all the things you can do when your nervousness shrinks! Read this book and follow its tips. Your confidence is just around the corner.

—Christine A. Padesky, PhD
Coauthor, *Mind Over Mood: Change How You Feel by Changing the Way You Think*
Director, Center for Cognitive Therapy
Huntington Beach, California

Introduction

Wouldn't it be nice if you could just flick a switch and make your shyness go away? No more worrying about what others think about you, no more embarrassment in front of other people. You could just relax and feel comfortable and confident, the way you probably think everyone else feels.

Unfortunately we can't get rid of anxiety altogether; it is part of human nature and we all have it. The oldest and most primitive part of the brain, popularly referred to as the reptile brain, is something we have in common with many other species. When the reptile brain senses danger, it activates a part of the nervous system, that causes us to experience anxious feelings. Without anxiety we would take unnecessary risks.

Our nervous systems are designed to help us know when we need to be alert in social situations. Almost everybody feels a little nervous starting a conversation with someone they don't know or asking a question in class, and teens who are shy feel anxiety during social interactions like these. Some teens are socially anxious, which means they experience such high anxiety that they avoid social situations. If you feel like your anxiety has you on the wrong end of the leash, then this book is for you.

Chapter 1: Socially Anxious
Are You Missing Out?

When you are at school, a restaurant, or a party, do you worry that people might think something you do is stupid or dumb? Do you think that people might laugh at you? Do you worry that you might do something that will make you feel ashamed or embarrassed? If so, you might be among the one in twenty teens who suffer from social anxiety.

Being concerned about being observed by others and negatively judged is normal for teenagers. Most everybody has experienced feeling nervous, scared, panicky, insecure, embarrassed, or ashamed in social or performance situations.

Introducing Liz, Alex, Bella, and Brandon, four socially anxious teens who will help you understand social anxiety and learn what you can do about it.

2

Here are some common situations that can trigger social anxiety. Check off each situation that makes you anxious.

- [ ] Answering or talking on the telephone
- [ ] Answering questions in class
- [ ] Asking someone out
- [ ] Asking the teacher a question or for help
- [ ] Attending parties, dances, or school activities
- [ ] Blushing, shaking, or sweating in front of others
- [ ] Eating in front of others
- [ ] Entering a room where others are already seated
- [ ] Giving a report or reading aloud in front of the class
- [ ] Going on a date
- [ ] Having your picture taken
- [ ] Inviting a friend to get together
- [ ] Participating in P.E. class
- [ ] Performing in public
- [ ] Speaking to adults
- [ ] Starting or joining a conversation
- [ ] Taking a test
- [ ] Talking to new or unfamiliar people
- [ ] Texting
- [ ] Using school or public bathrooms
- [ ] Walking in the hallways or hanging out by your locker
- [ ] Working with a group of teens
- [ ] Writing on the whiteboard or chalkboard

You probably identified with several of these trigger situations. Does that mean you are socially anxious? Not necessarily. It is normal for teens to feel anxious and awkward a lot of the time. Many social problems resolve themselves with time and experience.

The real test is not whether you feel anxious in a situation . . .

. . . but whether you go out of your way to avoid that situation.

You can live with social anxiety by avoiding situations that make you uncomfortable, but if that were working for you, you wouldn't be reading this book.

Chapter 2:

Why Me?
The Origins of Social Anxiety

Anxiety is a tool that we need for survival—what scientists call an adaptation. We've been using the primitive part of our brains, our reptile brains, for thousands of years to protect us from threats as varied as a charging wild boar to crossing a busy intersection.

We need anxiety in the same way a house needs a smoke detector: to alert us to danger. But if you are a socially anxious teen, your personal smoke detector is going off every time someone fries an egg or makes a piece of toast.

So why is **your** smoke detector so hypersensitive while other people's aren't? There are three causes of social anxiety. You might have one or you might have all three, but as you'll see, none of them are your fault.

Genetic Disposition

You didn't come up with this trait all by yourself. If you shake your family tree, you will likely find an uncle or a great-grandmother or even one of your parents who shows anxious traits similar to yours. They may not have had full-fledged social anxiety, but they were "dialed up" in a way you might recognize. Scientists haven't discovered a specific social anxiety gene yet, but just like blue eyes or curly hair, anxiety is passed down through generations.*

List any of your relatives who you know or suspect have anxiety in social situations.

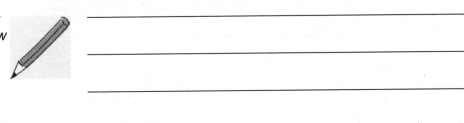

_____

_____

_____

_____

* In addition to shyness, there are a variety of other anxiety problems you or your relatives may have experienced. Appendix D at the end of the book lists these common anxieties.

Parent Modeling

Do your parents rarely socialize? Are they preoccupied with making good impressions? If your parents are overly cautious or shy themselves, their modeling could very well have contributed to your social anxiety.

 Describe any ways that your parents model anxiety and avoidance.

_____

_____

_____

_____

_____

Upsetting Events

Almost everyone has experienced forgetting their lines in a school presentation or play. For most people, the experience is a memory to chuckle over, but for the socially anxious it may have been a traumatic disaster. They are so worried about a repeat performance that being called upon in class or doing an oral presentation is genuinely terrifying.

Your own personal traumatic event could have been giving the wrong answer in class, finding out you weren't invited to a party when everyone else was, a rumor that you liked a classmate you really didn't, or a mean teacher who shamed you in front of the class.

 What upsetting events stand out in your memory?

_____

_____

_____

_____

_____

_____

_____

Unfortunately we can't undo the past, so your upsetting events, your parental models, and your genes are yours forever. The good news is that whatever the underlying cause of your shyness, the solution is the same. You can harness your anxieties—tweak your smoke detector—so that they work for you when you need them and stay out of the way when you don't.

The Chain Gang

Chapter 3: *Thoughts, Feelings, and Actions*

Scenario: Alex notices Ginelle, whom he finds attractive, approaching in the hall. He quickly buries his head in his locker and pretends to be looking for a book. Within a few seconds, Ginelle turns the corner and the danger has passed.

What actually happened here? If we are going to get a handle on social anxiety, we have to break it down so we can identify the links in the chain of events. Let's start with what we can observe: Alex's behavior. Alex stuck his head in his locker, apparently to avoid contact with someone he is actually attracted to. Is this in Alex's best interest? Why would Alex act in a way that reduces his chances of getting to know someone he likes?

If we asked him, Alex might have an explanation like "I needed a book in my locker," but if he's honest with himself and us he might say that he felt uncomfortable when he saw Ginelle. He might describe his discomfort with a word like "anxious," "panicky," "insecure," "embarrassed," or just plain "scared."

FEELING

In this book, when we talk about feelings we are talking about both your emotions and your physical reactions. Here are some common emotions that shy teens feel:

EMBARRASSED—foolish, humiliated, self-conscious

ANXIOUS—worried, panicky, nervous, frightened

INFERIOR—worthless, inadequate, defective, insecure

LONELY—unloved, unwanted, rejected, alone, abandoned

HOPELESS—discouraged, pessimistic, defeated

ASHAMED—remorseful, bad, guilty

SAD—blue, depressed, down, unhappy

FRUSTRATED—stuck, thwarted, defeated

JEALOUS—envious, distrustful

CONFUSED—befuddled, confounded, lost

HURT—wounded, upset, injured

DISAPPOINTED—let down, disillusioned, disheartened

ANGRY—mad, resentful, annoyed, irritated, upset, enraged

The other feelings we're talking about are sensations you experience in your body. These sensations are common with all kinds of anxiety, but especially important for people with social anxiety. Have you ever worried that people would notice your physical symptoms—like sweating, blushing, or having a shaky voice or hands—and negatively judge you? When you are afraid people might judge you, your mind sends a danger signal to your body. Your physical reactions may include:

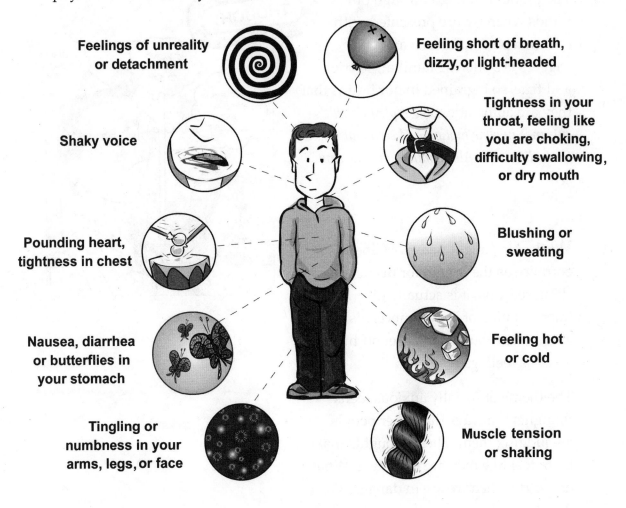

Feelings of unreality or detachment

Feeling short of breath, dizzy, or light-headed

Shaky voice

Tightness in your throat, feeling like you are choking, difficulty swallowing, or dry mouth

Pounding heart, tightness in chest

Blushing or sweating

Nausea, diarrhea or butterflies in your stomach

Feeling hot or cold

Tingling or numbness in your arms, legs, or face

Muscle tension or shaking

One thing to remember is that your physical symptoms of anxiety are much more obvious to you than they are to other people.

But what caused Alex's anxious feelings? What could make Alex feel like disappearing into thin air every time he sees Ginelle? We could ask him, but Alex may not even be aware of what goes on in his head during the nanosecond between Ginelle's surprise appearances and his hasty retreats. He might say, "I'm not really sure what I was thinking. Ginelle always makes me feel this way."

The thoughts that go through our minds when we are presented with our own personal social anxiety triggers are often so familiar, so tried and true, so ingrained in our brains that they are automatic. *Let's replay Ginelle's entrance in slow motion and see what flashed through Alex's mind when he saw her.*

While Alex might perceive Ginelle's entrance as the trigger for his personal chain reaction, it is actually his interpretation of her entrance, his **automatic thoughts**, that set off his anxious feelings.

The theme of socially anxious teens' thoughts is always that other people are judging them. These thoughts make them feel like they are in danger. What do we do when we are in danger? We do what we've done ever since the first caveman confronted a mountain lion: run away and hide!

When people face situations that make them anxious, avoidance is the most common action they take. Avoidance prevents the thing that they are afraid will happen from happening.

Alex is afraid he won't know what to say to Ginelle. If he hides in his locker, there is no risk of this happening. It's a foolproof short-term solution. The problem? In the long run, Alex never gets what he really wants, which is to get to know Ginelle better. He winds up feeling isolated, discouraged, and depressed.

If you let your reptile brain lead the way, it will lead you astray.

Automatic thoughts, anxious feelings, and avoidance behavior are the three links in the chain of events that make up social anxiety.

Let's look at some typical scenes in the lives of Liz, Bella, and two other socially anxious teens, Chris and Elisha.

Liz

Let's review Liz's thought-feeling-action chain in this situation.

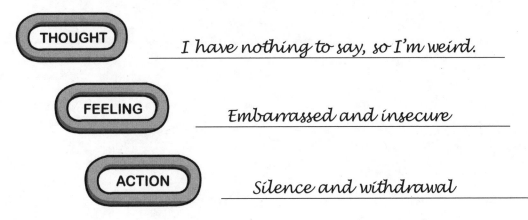

THOUGHT _I have nothing to say, so I'm weird._

FEELING _Embarrassed and insecure_

ACTION _Silence and withdrawal_

Have you ever been with a group of people who are conversing about something you don't know much about?

 What were you afraid might happen?

_____

_____

 What were you feeling at the time?

_____

ACTION What did you do?

_____

_____

Bella

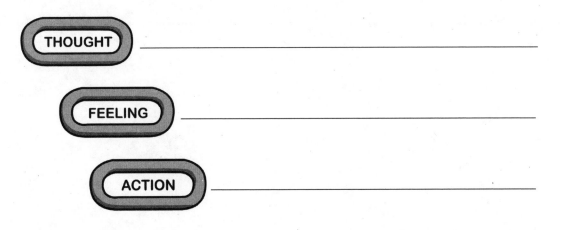

Can you describe Bella's thought-feeling-action chain in this situation?

THOUGHT _____

FEELING _____

ACTION _____

Think about times when you have to introduce yourself.

 What are you typically thinking in those situations?

_____

_____

 What are you typically feeling? Describe any physical signs of anxiety you are afraid others might notice.

_____

 When you feel that way and are worried that someone might notice visible signs of your anxiety, what do you tend to do?

_____

Chris

Here's a situation that triggers Chris's anxiety. He thinks he's strange, but many teens share similar thoughts and feelings.

Write down Chris's thought-feeling-action chain.

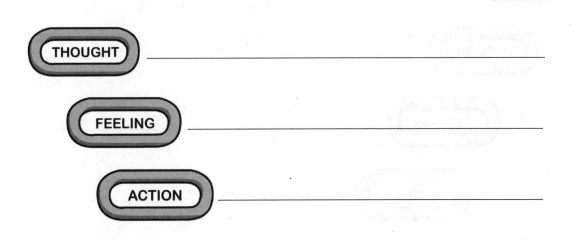

THOUGHT _____

FEELING _____

ACTION _____

Elisha

ELISHA IS EATING LUNCH IN A VIRTUALLY EMPTY FOOD COURT WHEN A GROUP OF FRIENDS FROM SCHOOL APPEAR AND JOIN HER AT THE TABLE.

THEY'RE GOING TO WATCH ME EAT.

I'LL DISGUST THEM!

SUDDENLY SHE FEELS SELF-CONSCIOUS. HER STOMACH CLENCHES, HER MOUTH DRIES UP, AND SHE LOSES HER APPETITE.

CAN I HAVE ONE OF THESE?

HELP YOURSELF. I'M NOT HUNGRY.

What is Elisha's thought-feeling-action chain?

THOUGHT _____

FEELING _____

ACTION _____

Like Chris and Elisha, you may find it very hard to do certain activities in the presence of others even though you do them perfectly naturally when you are alone. Think of a situation or activity that makes you feel self-conscious.

 What are you afraid others might think of you?

_____

_____

 How do you feel when you find yourself in this situation?

_____

_____

 What action goes along with these thoughts and feelings?

_____

_____

The thought-feeling-action chain happens quickly in anxious situations, so quickly that it often seems beyond our control and we feel helpless to stop it. Does that mean you are doomed to a life of everlasting avoidance? Certainly not!

A chain is only as strong as its weakest link. Let's take a closer look at your chain reactions. If you can identify the links, you can strategize how to go about breaking the chain. Go back to the list on page 3 and look at the situations you checked as those that make you anxious. Choose the two that make you most anxious, and see if you can label each link—thought, feeling, and action—in the space below.

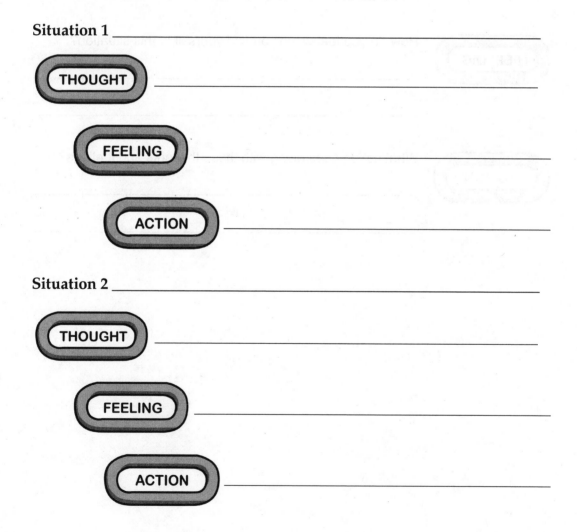

Situation 1 _____

(THOUGHT) _____

(FEELING) _____

(ACTION) _____

Situation 2 _____

(THOUGHT) _____

(FEELING) _____

(ACTION) _____

Chapter 4: **Disastrous Distortions**
Don't Believe Every Thought You Think

Imagine you are looking at yourself in a funhouse mirror at a carnival or fair. Yes, that is you, but your face is not that long, your stomach is not that fat, and your legs are not that skinny. The mirror is distorting the reality of what is there.

When we are anxious, our thoughts get reflected in a funhouse mirror. Worse still, we are unaware of the distortion and take those thoughts at face value, making us even more scared.

This chapter explains six thinking mistakes, or distortions, that people with social anxiety commonly make. When you recognize the distortion in your thoughts, it becomes easier to take them less seriously.

Catastrophic Thinking

You've probably heard people ask, "What's the worst that can happen?" When a trigger situation occurs, and your mind jumps to the worst possible outcome—even though there are a hundred other possible outcomes—you are using catastrophic thinking.

When this teen is turned down for a date, he assumes it is so newsworthy that the whole school will soon know and be laughing at him. That might qualify as a catastrophe, but is it likely to happen?

Describe a situation in your own life where you used catastrophic thinking.

_____

_____

_____

What was the worst possible outcome that you assumed would happen?

_____

_____

_____

Discounting the Positive

When something good happens to you, do you chalk it up to luck? When somebody praises you, do you assume the person was just trying to be nice? Say you were talking to someone and, instead of getting all tongue-tied, you actually enjoyed the conversation. Instead of feeling good that sometimes you really do have something to talk about, you conclude, "Well, she's really nice, and that's why I felt comfortable, but most people aren't like that and I'd totally freeze up talking with them."

It is difficult to develop confidence when you ignore your successes, when you discount the positive.

Here's Cyndi, who has a nice voice, yet doubts her abilities in her choral class.

Have you ever been given a compliment you didn't feel you deserved? Write it down.

_____

_____

How did you discount the compliment?

_____

_____

28

People who see the good in everything are sometimes said to be wearing rose-colored glasses. A socially anxious teen in a trigger situation could be said to be wearing gray-colored glasses. All her senses are working and she is taking everything in, but she discounts all the information that is positive, leaving only the negative.

In what situations do you seem able to see only what isn't working?

_____

_____

Labeling

Sticks and stones may break your bones, but words can really harm you. By calling someone else names, you are degrading that person. Calling yourself names degrades you. For example, you drop your books in the hall, and you tell yourself you are lame. But we have all made clumsy mistakes. Are we all lame?

Losing a game of chess doesn't make you a loser. Blurting out a silly idea doesn't make you an idiot. Words like "lame" and "loser" and "idiot" are labels that don't really explain who you are.

Socially anxious teens often use labels like these to describe themselves. Which do you use on yourself?

☐ Pathetic
☐ Stupid
☐ Hopeless
☐ Defective
☐ Incompetent
☐ Idiot

☐ Boring
☐ Jerk
☐ Loser
☐ Lame
☐ Disgusting
☐ Mentally ill

Spotlighting

When a great golfer is driving the ball off the tee in a close match, she isn't thinking about her grip on the club or the arc of her stroke. An actor on stage doesn't watch his hands as he gestures, nor does he listen to his voice as he speaks his lines. The golfer and the actor want to lose themselves in their roles, not reflect on the mechanics of their performances.

So it is with us in our daily lives. When we turn the spotlight of attention onto ourselves, we become self-conscious. What should be natural and spontaneous self-expression becomes an agonizing performance. Spotlighting makes you feel different and separate from others. Everything you say starts to sound odd or fake. You don't trust or like how you are coming across, and to make matters worse, you assume everyone else is watching you as closely as you are watching yourself. How can you get into the flow of life and connect with others when you are preoccupied with what is going on inside yourself?

Everyone feels self-conscious from time to time, but most people notice it happening and let it go. They flick a switch and turn the spotlight off. But when socially anxious teens feel self-conscious, they dial the spotlight up, increasing their self-awareness to the point where they are paralyzed.

You can spotlight what is going on in your body as well. If you are sweating, shaking, or blushing, and you focus your attention on that, these normal signs of anxiety intensify. For example, when you are speaking in class you may notice that your heart is beating fast. Then, as you focus your attention on your heartbeat, the pounding intensifies until it feels like your heart might jump right out of your chest. "Everyone around me can see what's happening," you think to yourself. "They know I'm freaking out!"

As you leave the room after class, the spotlight follows you, showing everybody how awkwardly you walk. And so it goes throughout the day when you are living in the spotlight.

Describe a situation where you feel as if you are in the spotlight.

_____

_____

How do you imagine you are coming across to others?

_____

_____

What feelings do you have that you're sure people around you must see?

_____

_____

Mind Reading

If you feel like you are in a spotlight and everyone is watching you, it's only natural for you to also worry that everyone is thinking about you. As a mind reader, you assume you know what people are thinking, especially when it is something bad about you. You haven't any psychic powers, but somehow you just know.

And because you are so certain, you don't bother to check out what is actually happening. For example, you are hanging out with a friend who suddenly becomes distracted. Since you are a mind reader you know that your friend was bored and looking for an excuse to move on.

Describe an interaction you had with someone that made you anxious.

_____

_____

What did you think that person was thinking about you?

_____

_____

Social Perfectionism

For the social perfectionist, there are only two categories: either you are brilliant, funny, smart, and popular or you are dull, boring, stupid, and an outcast. There is simply no such thing as being okay or good enough. If you aren't invited to every party, then nobody likes you. If people do not listen with rapt attention every time you open your mouth to speak, you are boring.

When your idea of normal is everyone's approving of you all the time, you've set the bar too high, and you'll never clear it. Nobody is socially perfect, and thinking you can be will only lead to shame.

Here's how social perfectionism works in your brain:

Because *I told a bad joke*, I am *not funny*.

Fill in the blank perfectionist thought.

Because *someone laughed at my coat*, I _____.

Because *he didn't ask me out again*, I _____.

Because *she didn't text me back*, I _____.

Now try this exercise with your own perfectionist thoughts.

Because _____, I _____

_____.

Because _____, I _____

_____.

Because _____, I _____

_____.

Social perfectionism allows no room for error. It's a ruthless way to judge yourself, yet it is the most universal distortion and the most damaging for shy teens. In the next chapter, we're going to take an even closer look at this disastrous distortion.

Chapter 5:

The Values Compass
*Stepping Off the
Perfectionist Path
to Nowhere*

Remember the close relationship between thoughts, feelings, and actions? Social perfectionism becomes a problem when it makes you feel so anxious that you want to avoid situations. And the problem is even greater if those situations are ones that are important to you.

This rating exercise can give you a clue to your level of social perfectionism. Evaluate each statement on a scale from 1 to 5. Use 1 = disagree strongly and 5 = agree strongly.

When I tell a joke, it should be funny to everyone. _____

If I stumble on a word, people will think that there is something wrong with me. _____

If I say something that turns out to be wrong, people will think I am stupid. _____

If I forget people's names, they will think I don't care about them. _____

If someone criticizes what I am wearing, I have bad taste in clothing. _____

Awkward silences don't happen in normal conversations. _____

If I say something that someone takes the wrong way, I am insensitive. _____

When giving an oral presentation, I should be relaxed and confident. _____

If I appear nervous (for example, I blush or shake), others will see me as weak. _____

Total _____

How did your answers add up? Your total isn't a scientific measurement, but generally speaking the higher you scored, the more likely it is that you don't allow yourself any slack in social situations. Any effort you make to connect with others that isn't received with a 100 percent positive reaction is considered a failure. This is social perfectionism, one of the disastrous distortions from chapter 4, and it is shared by nearly all shy people.

Right now you may be saying to yourself: "Those statements don't sound like perfectionism, they sound realistic. I'm not a perfectionist. Perfectionists are overachievers, people who believe that nothing less than an A+ is good enough, right?"

By not allowing any possibility of failure in your social actions, you are expecting yourself to always be interesting, relaxed, funny, smart, or whatever you think you should be. You are setting a higher standard for yourself than for others who are not so shy. It is this high standard, an impossibly perfect standard to maintain, that is making you feel more anxious.

Social perfectionists are setting an impossible standard for themselves.

Social perfectionists perceive others as being perfect, but of course nobody is. Everybody has moments of awkwardness and even times when they fail outright. So how do you get a reality check on this standard? One way is to look around you at the behavior of others. Observing others can sometimes give you a more realistic view of how people normally act—they may not be as perfect as you think. What you learn by watching them may help you lower the expectations you place on yourself.

During the next week or so, watch your friends or acquaintances in the following situations and rate them on a scale from 1 to 5.

Telling a joke

| 0 | 1 | 2 | 3 | 4 | 5 |

Not funny at all   *Hilarious*

Talking about a subject

| 0 | 1 | 2 | 3 | 4 | 5 |

Totally dumb   *Super smart*

Making conversation

| 0 | 1 | 2 | 3 | 4 | 5 |

Completely boring   *Really interesting*

How they look

| 0 | 1 | 2 | 3 | 4 | 5 |

Extremely insecure   *Very calm and confident*

Your True Values

What's important to you? Is it not making mistakes? Having everyone like you? Never being rejected? Social perfectionism is what most shy people fixate on, acting as if it were what life is all about.

Alex avoids talking with girls he is attracted to because he's afraid that he won't have anything clever to say or that he will say something painfully boring or weird. Are the most important things in his life that he never say anything weird, or that he never be the cause of an awkward silence in a conversation? If avoiding those conversational pitfalls is so crucial to Alex's happiness, why isn't he happier? He's certainly done a good job of avoiding them. To help Alex figure out what his true values are—what really matters most in life to him—let's have him try the following exercise.

Alex imagines that he is at his twenty-first birthday party. He pictures someone who knows and cares about him: a friend, a romantic partner, or a coworker. This person is telling everyone at the party how he or she feels about him. What words or phrases would Alex like to hear used to describe himself?

"What's so cool about Alex is that he's so fun and spontaneous. He's a risk taker."

Now he pictures himself at his thirtieth birthday party. He imagines the person he is closest with. What would that person say he stands for?

"You're the most important person in my life because you're the most honest, reliable friend a person could have."

Now Alex is at his fiftieth birthday party. He pictures someone who knows and cares about him. What about Alex does this person admire?

"I've always looked up to you because you are true to yourself. You do the right thing no matter what."

Let's look at the words and phrases Alex would like people to use to describe his character.

- fun and spontaneous
- risk taker
- honest
- reliable
- true to himself
- does the right thing

These are more than just words to Alex. These are his true values. When Alex sticks his head in his locker to avoid meeting Ginelle, is he living according to any of these values?

It's Your Turn!

Now try this exercise thinking about yourself. Close your eyes, and imagine your birthday party in the future. Picture someone who knows and cares about you. It could be someone that you know now or that you imagine you might know in the future: a friend, a romantic partner, a husband or wife, or a child you may have someday. This person is telling everyone at the party how he or she feels about you. What words or phrases would you like to hear used to describe you?

 On your twenty-first birthday: What's so cool about you is …

_____

_____

 On your thirtieth birthday: You're the most important person in my life because …

_____

_____

 On your fiftieth birthday: I've always looked up to you because …

_____

_____

The words and phrases that you imagined other people said about you reflect personal qualities that are important to you. They show how you want to be in the world. These are your true values.

 Write down these words and phrases here:

_____

_____

You will use this list of values to help guide your behavior in future exercises in this book.

Your values can act as a compass in life. They can help you move in the direction that you know in your heart you want to move in. Imagine that you are on a boat in the sea of life. North is toward your values. South is toward perfectionism and avoidance. When you move south, you may feel safer, but you will not end up where you truly want to go.

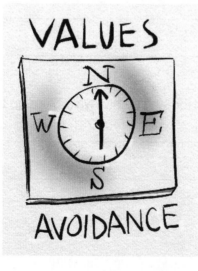

What Was I Thinking?
*Fact-Checking and the
Values Test*

Chapter 6:

If what we think determines how we feel, and
if how we feel guides our actions, then our
thoughts, being the first link in the chain, play
a pretty important role in our lives. Our success
and happiness are riding on those thoughts, but can we always believe
them? There are many different ways to interpret the situations we find
ourselves in.

On the next page let's look at how three
different thoughts about one situation can spark
three different sets of feelings and actions.

48

You may very well be wondering, "So how do I know what thoughts to trust? How do I know what to believe?" These are good questions. The answer is that we can't really know for sure. A better question is, how do we evaluate the various thoughts that drive our actions?

There are two ways to evaluate a thought. The first way is to check the accuracy of the thought by looking for distortions. The second way is to examine what that thought leads you to feel and ultimately do. Does that action move you toward or away from what you value?

Remember Elisha eating in the mall food court in chapter 3? She was eating lunch alone when a group of her friends happened by. Let's retrace her thought-feeling-action chain, this time identifying the disastrous distortion that set it off, and the result of the action; did it take her toward avoidance or toward more important personal values?

Anxious Thoughts	Distortions	Feelings	Actions	Toward Avoidance or Values?
"They're going to watch me eat."	spotlighting	self-consciousness	stop eating immediately	avoidance
"I'll disgust them."	mind reading, labeling	shame	avoid any social situation that might involve eating	avoidance

Of course, we don't actually know what Elisha's personal values are, but it's a good bet turning down social situations that might involve eating will make her less connected and more alone.

Let's do this exercise with Liz, who thinks she's a boring conversationalist.

Anxious Thoughts	Distortions	Feelings	Actions	Toward Avoidance or Values?
"I don't have anything to say."	social perfectionism	self-consciousness	be quiet	avoidance
"They are noticing how quiet I am."	mind reading, spotlighting	embarrassment	don't speak unless spoken to	avoidance
"They think I'm weird."	labeling	self-consciousness	withdraw from conversation	avoidance

What does Liz's withdrawal from the conversation tell us about the reliability of the thoughts that drove her action?

Remember Bella, the girl introducing herself to a group? Let's break it down for her.

Anxious Thoughts	Distortions	Feelings	Actions	Toward Avoidance or Values?
"When it is my turn to talk, my face will turn beet red."	spotlighting, catastrophic thinking, social perfectionism	self-consciousness	lower head, pull up turtleneck	avoidance
"Everyone will see how anxious I am."	spotlighting, social perfectionism	embarrassment	cover face to hide blushing	avoidance

Take a look at a personal situation that makes you anxious. If you need ideas, go back to the chain reactions you filled in on page 24.

Situation	
Anxious Thoughts	
Distortions	What distorted thinking does your anxious prediction rely on? ☐ **Catastrophic thinking** (assuming the worst possible outcome) ☐ **Discounting the positive** (refusing to take credit when you deserve it) ☐ **Labeling** (putting a negative name on yourself) ☐ **Spotlighting** (thinking everybody is watching you and/or how you feel inside shows on the outside) ☐ **Mind reading** (guessing what others are thinking or will think) ☐ **Social perfectionism** (setting a standard for yourself that doesn't allow for mistakes)
Feelings	
Actions	
Toward Avoidance or Values?	

You're on a roll; let's do a couple more.

Situation	
Anxious Thoughts	
Distortions	What distorted thinking does your anxious prediction rely on? ☐ **Catastrophic thinking** (assuming the worst possible outcome) ☐ **Discounting the positive** (refusing to take credit when you deserve it) ☐ **Labeling** (putting a negative name on yourself) ☐ **Spotlighting** (thinking everybody is watching you and/or how you feel inside shows on the outside) ☐ **Mind reading** (guessing what others are thinking or will think) ☐ **Social perfectionism** (setting a standard for yourself that doesn't allow for mistakes)
Feelings	
Actions	
Toward Avoidance or Values?	

Situation	
Anxious Thoughts	
Distortions	What distorted thinking does your anxious prediction rely on? ☐ **Catastrophic thinking** (assuming the worst possible outcome) ☐ **Discounting the positive** (refusing to take credit when you deserve it) ☐ **Labeling** (putting a negative name on yourself) ☐ **Spotlighting** (thinking everybody is watching you and/or how you feel inside shows on the outside) ☐ **Mind reading** (guessing what others are thinking or will think) ☐ **Social perfectionism** (setting a standard for yourself that doesn't allow for mistakes)
Feelings	
Actions	
Toward Avoidance or Values?	

By now you are probably thinking, "Okay, I get the point. My anxious automatic thoughts aren't necessarily true, and they are making me do stuff that isn't helping me move toward my values. But I can't just block them out, can I? I can't simply not think them!"

Chapter 7: **Talking Back to Your Thoughts**
Training Your Brain to Challenge and Cope

Ever try not to think of a banana? It doesn't have to be a banana—it could be any word—but for argument's sake, let's try it with "banana." For the next thirty seconds, don't think about a banana.

. . . 27 . . . 28 . . . 29 . . . 30.

How did that work for you? Fact is, trying to push thoughts out of our minds won't get rid of them; in fact, it can make them come up more often. Changes in our thinking are usually caused by changes in our experience. But as long as you believe your same old anxious thoughts, you are not likely to have new experiences.

If we want to try new things, to gain new experience, to move toward our values, we need to challenge our anxious thoughts—not block or wipe them out—but challenge them with reasonable questions.

What sort of questions might Alex have asked himself when he was faced with Ginelle?

Alex's anxious thought: "I won't know what to say."

Distortion: Social perfectionism

His challenge question: "Do I know for certain that I won't have anything to say?"

Alex's anxious thought: "Ginelle will think I'm weird."

Distortion: Labeling

His challenge question: "Does not saying something clever equal being weird?"

Alex's anxious thought: "If I embarrass myself in front of her, she will talk to all her friends about how weird I am, and then the whole school will think I am weird."

Distortion: Catastrophic thinking

His challenge question: "What is more likely to happen? How could I cope with that?"

And after the experience . . .

Alex's anxious thought: "She barely recognized me. All she did was say hi."

Distortion: Discounting the positive

His challenge question: "What did I do that was okay?"

The answers to challenge questions become your coping thoughts. Let's see what coping thoughts Alex came up with:

Alex's challenge question: "Do I know for certain that I won't have anything to say?"

His coping thoughts: "I might be able to think of something to say. I'm pretty sure I can smile and say hi. That's something."

Alex's challenge question: "Does not saying something clever equal being weird?"

His coping thoughts: "When other people don't know what to say, I don't think they are weird. She may not think I'm weird either."

Alex's challenge question: "What is more likely to happen? How could I cope with that?"

His coping thoughts: "Ginelle might not even look at me. She could act all rude and stuck up. If that happened, I could talk it over with a friend and at least I would know she's not for me."

And after the experience . . .

Alex's challenge question: "What did I do that was okay?"

His coping thoughts: "I was assertive. I walked right up to her and said hi. I proved to myself that I'm braver than I thought. Now she knows I exist and I have a chance of getting to know her better."

Fill in the following chart based on one of your own anxious thoughts. Feel free to use these challenge questions.

Catastrophic thinking: What is more likely to happen? How could I cope with it?

Discounting the positive: What did I do that was okay?

Labeling: Does this word apply to me all the time in every situation?

Spotlighting: What else might everyone be paying attention to besides me? Do people really care that much about what I am doing?

Mind reading: What evidence do I have that this is what people are thinking?

Social perfectionism: Am I asking more of myself than I would of others?

Anxious Thought	
Distortions	What distorted thinking does your anxious prediction rely on? ☐ **Catastrophic thinking** (assuming the worst possible outcome) ☐ **Discounting the positive** (refusing to take credit when you deserve it) ☐ **Labeling** (putting a negative name on yourself) ☐ **Spotlighting** (thinking everybody is watching you and/or how you feel inside shows on the outside) ☐ **Mind reading** (guessing what others are thinking or will think) ☐ **Social perfectionism** (setting a standard for yourself that doesn't allow for mistakes)
Challenge Question	
Coping Thought	

Remember the thought-feeling-action chain? Each new coping thought you come up with gives you an alternative to the automatic anxious thoughts you've been using for so long. The good news is, with practice and persistence, coping thoughts will help you face your fears, and facing your fears will give you new experiences that will create new ways of thinking.

Chapter 8: ## The Exposure Ladder
From Avoidance to Action

Alex has done some good work. He's defined his values, and he understands how avoiding scary situations takes him further from getting what he wants. He's identified the automatic thoughts that drive his anxious feelings and avoidance behavior. He's examined those thoughts for distortions and challenged them with coping questions. He should be okay now, right? Shouldn't his avoidance behavior pretty well have disappeared for him, and for you too, if you've been doing the work in this book?

Not so fast. Coping thoughts won't simply replace your distorted anxious thoughts. Reasoning won't kill them. Like vampires, these thoughts will live forever unless they are exposed to sunlight. To really change the way we think, we need to purposely experience what we've been avoiding. We need exposure. Exposure is moving toward your fears instead of away from them. By facing your fears repeatedly you will learn to manage them and move on.

For Alex to gain confidence in himself, he's going to have to actually talk to Ginelle.

Alex knows what situation is important to him—any situation with Ginelle. He's avoiding the very person he is most attracted to, and he's sick and tired of it. Alex needs to turn his avoidance situation into an exposure.

Take a moment to choose your own avoidance situation to transform into an exposure. Consider each situation in this chart. Rate it for scariness, and check the box that, given your values, best indicates how important each situation is for you. At the bottom of the list is a blank line where you can write a situation of your own.

Avoidance Situation	Scariness Rating (1–10)	Very Important	Important	Not Important
Answering or talking on the telephone				
Answering questions in class				
Asking someone out				
Asking the teacher a question or for help				
Attending parties, dances, or school activities				
Blushing, shaking, or sweating in front of others				
Eating in front of others				
Entering a room where others are already seated				
Giving a report or reading aloud in front of the class				
Going on a date				
Having your picture taken				
Inviting a friend to get together				
Participating in P.E. class				
Performing in public				
Speaking to adults				
Starting or joining a conversation				
Taking a test				
Talking to new or unfamiliar people				
Texting				
Using school or public bathrooms				
Walking in the hallways or hanging out by your locker				
Working with a group of teens				
Writing on the whiteboard or chalkboard				

Now that you've identified which of the situations you've been avoiding are important to you, let's pick one to work on. It should be a situation that reflects your values. You are going to turn that avoidance situation into an exposure. "Expose myself to the very thing I've been avoiding?" you may say. "I could never do that."

Don't worry; you won't be starting off on the high dive. You'll begin at the shallow end of the pool.

Let's look at the avoidance situation Alex chose: asking Ginelle out on a date. It was very important to him, and he rated it as a 10 in scariness (on a scale of 1 to 10). Exposing himself to that level of embarrassment seemed an impossible goal, certainly not something he could accomplish all at once. Alex put this new exposure situation at the top of his ladder, with rungs of smaller, less scary steps leading up to it. This is Alex's exposure ladder.

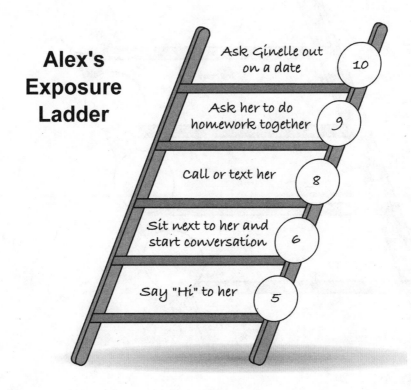

Alex's Exposure Ladder

Ask Ginelle out on a date — 10

Ask her to do homework together — 9

Call or text her — 8

Sit next to her and start conversation — 6

Say "Hi" to her — 5

Let's put Alex on hold for a moment and get back to you. On the top rung of the ladder that follows, write the situation you'd like to face. On the bottom rung, write the least scary step you can think of that would lead in that direction. For example, if your top rung is to give a presentation in class, your bottom rung might be to tell a joke to a friend. One by one, fill in the rungs of your ladder so that each exposure builds on the one before. Take your time building your ladder; you're going to need it for the rest of this book.

If you need ideas, here are several sample ladders built for common avoidance/exposure situations. The order of the rungs would probably be different for each person completing the ladder, so rate how scary each exposure is for you by putting a number from 1 to 10 in the circle.

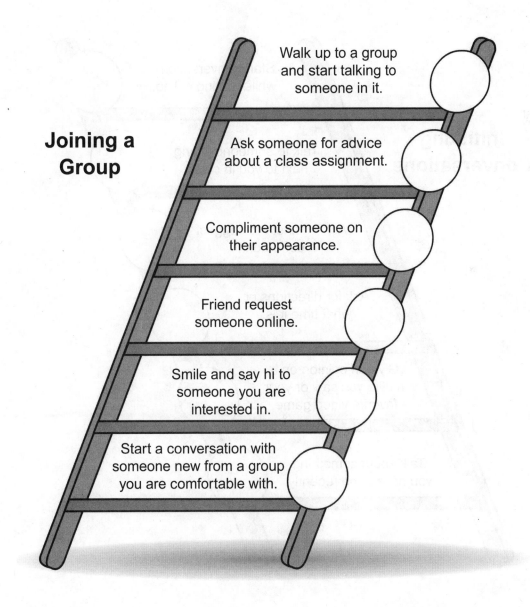

Joining a Group

Walk up to a group and start talking to someone in it.

Ask someone for advice about a class assignment.

Compliment someone on their appearance.

Friend request someone online.

Smile and say hi to someone you are interested in.

Start a conversation with someone new from a group you are comfortable with.

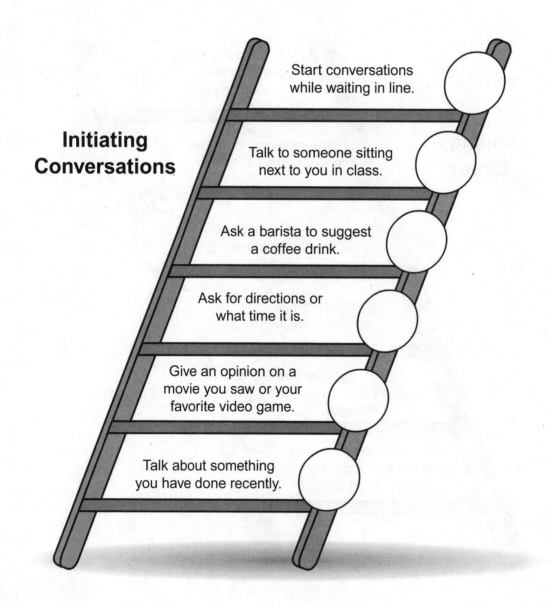

Initiating Conversations

Start conversations while waiting in line.

Talk to someone sitting next to you in class.

Ask a barista to suggest a coffee drink.

Ask for directions or what time it is.

Give an opinion on a movie you saw or your favorite video game.

Talk about something you have done recently.

Dating

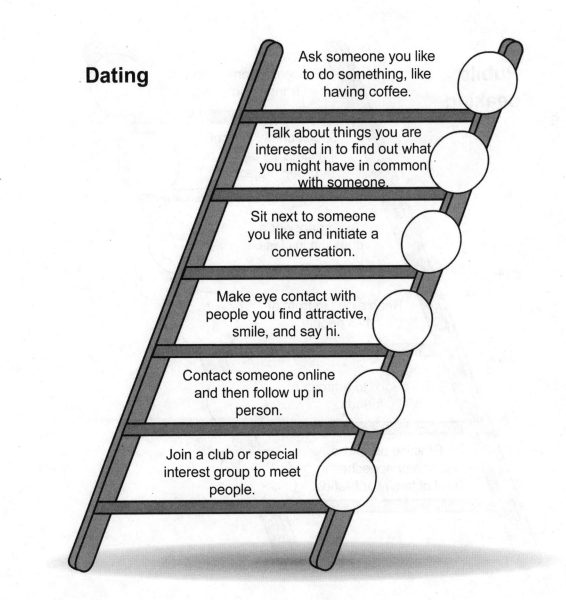

Ask someone you like to do something, like having coffee.

Talk about things you are interested in to find out what you might have in common with someone.

Sit next to someone you like and initiate a conversation.

Make eye contact with people you find attractive, smile, and say hi.

Contact someone online and then follow up in person.

Join a club or special interest group to meet people.

Public Speaking

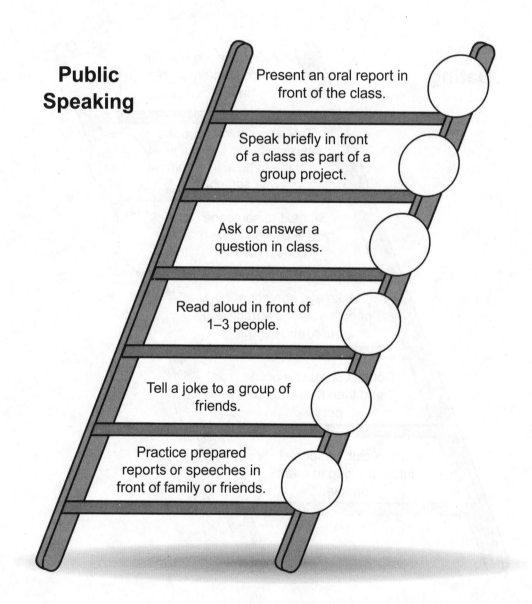

Present an oral report in front of the class.

Speak briefly in front of a class as part of a group project.

Ask or answer a question in class.

Read aloud in front of 1–3 people.

Tell a joke to a group of friends.

Practice prepared reports or speeches in front of family or friends.

Grab a Rung!
Getting a Grip on Your Exposure Ladder

Chapter 9:

Have you completed your exposure ladder? Great—good work! Chances are, you are not exactly jumping at the opportunity to do your first exposure. You may have tried something similar in the past and regretted it. This time, you're going to need a new strategy, better support, and a more accurate way to judge the results. Let's follow along with Alex as he prepares for his bottom rung by filling out this exposure chart.

Alex begins by naming the exposure, or situation he has been avoiding, that he is now planning to face—the lowest rung on his ladder, saying hi to Ginelle. The next row, his anxious prediction, is what he is afraid will happen—and probably feels absolutely certain will happen—when he exposes himself to the situation. Next is his perfectionist goal, an unrealistic expectation that only makes him more anxious. Social perfectionism allows no room for mistakes or surprises, and if Alex goes into his exposure with this goal in mind, he is doomed for failure.

Exposure	What feared situation are you facing? Saying hi to Ginelle
Anxious Prediction	What are you afraid will happen? I'll look nervous. She'll think I'm weird or creepy.
Perfectionist Goal	How do you think you should act and appear in this situation? Calm and confident

Alex's idea that he has to appear calm and confident around girls is unrealistic and only makes him more anxious.

Before Alex moves forward to the next part of the exposure chart, there is one more very important question he must answer, which has to do with his past behavior, not his thinking. The question is, what did he do to keep his anxious prediction from coming true?

Alex was once in a science class group project with Ginelle. He stayed in the group, and he even actually spoke to her once, but before he opened his mouth he mentally rehearsed everything he was going to say so it wouldn't sound dumb. He never looked directly at Ginelle, and he spoke only about the project itself, not about anything personal. The moment the conversation turned spontaneous, Alex fixed his eyes on his notes and waited until the crisis had passed.

What Alex did is called safety behavior, and it is another more subtle form of avoidance. Safety behaviors are what we do to keep the things we are afraid will happen from happening. It's like swimming with water wings on to keep yourself from drowning. Yes, you are in the water, but you're not really swimming. Water wings don't help you gain confidence in your own ability to stay afloat. You might always think the reason you did not drown was that you had your water wings on.

Here are some examples of safety behaviors:
- Calling a friend but thinking out what you are going to say first, or texting instead of calling
- Going to a party, but not initiating conversations
- Asking someone out, but not the person you are really interested in
- Going to school, but avoiding looking people in the eye
- Talking only to people who do not intimidate you
- Sitting in the back of the class so people cannot watch you
- Using alcohol or other drugs at social gatherings
- Never ordering things at restaurants that you are afraid you will mispronounce

Alex knew from past experience that when he was around girls he was attracted to he said only what he'd rehearsed and avoided eye contact. If he does that now with Ginelle, he won't be truly testing his anxious prediction, so he'd better write it down in the chart to help him remember what not to do.

Safety Behavior	What would you normally do to prevent your anxious prediction from happening?
	Avoid eye contact, rehearse what I'm going to say.

Alex has identified correctly what's been wrong with his thinking and behavior in this situation. The next section of the chart is designed for Alex to outline the new thinking that will help him stop avoiding. Taking the time to reflect on these questions and write answers is crucial to a successful exposure.

Anxious Prediction	What is your anxious prediction? *I'll look nervous and Ginelle will think I'm weird or creepy.*
Distortions	What distorted thinking does your anxious prediction rely on? ☐ **Catastrophic thinking** (assuming the worst possible outcome) ☐ **Discounting the positive** (refusing to take credit when you deserve it) ☑ **Labeling** (putting a negative name on yourself) ☐ **Spotlighting** (thinking everybody is watching you and/or how you feel inside shows on the outside) ☑ **Mind reading** (guessing what others are thinking or will think) ☐ **Social perfectionism** (setting a standard for yourself that doesn't allow for mistakes)
Coping Thought	What can you remind yourself of when you are feeling the most anxious? *I am just being friendly. If she reacts negatively to me, I can cope with that. She may not even be the girl for me.*
Realistic Goal	What can you accomplish even though you feel anxious? *Smiling, looking her in the eye, trying to start a conversation*
Values	What motivates you to move in this direction? *Being true to myself*

Because he has questioned his automatic thoughts, Alex can identify the distortions in them and recognize that his anxious prediction won't necessarily come true. His coping thought is a direct answer to his distorted anxious thoughts above. His realistic goal is what he will use to replace his perfectionist one; it is the observable behavior he reasonably hopes to accomplish even though he may feel anxiety while accomplishing it. The goal may be simply to not resort to safety behaviors. If Alex walks up to Ginelle, looks at her, and says hi, he gets an A+.

To complete the chart, the most important question Alex can ask himself is "What personal value is driving me in this direction?" He'll need to have that ready in his mind when the going gets rough; it is the compass that will keep him on course.

But as Alex prepares, his anxious thoughts start to intensify, getting louder and more persistent. His body reacts, with his heart beating faster, his face getting hot, his muscles tensing, and his hands shaking. His mind is telling him not to do it, that she will think he is an idiot and he won't have anything to say. It will be obvious to Ginelle how nervous he is, which will make her think he is weak and weird. If he listens to his thoughts right now, he'll stick his head in the locker.

If Alex is going to go through with this exposure, he's going to have to do it with the same old drumbeat of anxious thoughts that have been playing in his head for years every time an attractive girl is around. He's sick of that soundtrack; he knows it's not for him, but when it's blasting away it makes him feel anxious, and when he feels anxious his feet move him away from his values.

The bottom line is that, like Alex, you have to decide who is going to be the boss: your reptile brain or you. You won't move toward your values if you give all your attention to your doubts and fears. In life, as well as sports, we win by keeping our eyes and ears on the prize.

When the drumbeat of anxiety doesn't go away, you'll have to focus on your coping thoughts, and, as the Nike slogan says, "Just do it."

Well, that was awkward! As the anxious thoughts and feelings fade away, Alex sighs with relief. And we might well be wondering, was it worth it? Would Alex have been better off simply avoiding all that pain?

True, Ginelle didn't smile brightly and fall in love with Alex on the spot. She couldn't even remember his name. Alex isn't really sure what she thinks about him now; she might even be laughing at him.

After any exposure or any social interaction, shy people often begin obsessing about what they may have done wrong. Thoughts like "I should have said . . ." and "Why didn't I . . .?" echo in their heads. Replaying what they should have done is more perfectionist thinking. Nobody can meet that standard, and if Alex evaluates his experience on those terms he'll feel like a failure and go back to avoiding Ginelle.

The important things for Alex to ask himself are "Did I meet my realistic goal?" and "Did I move toward my values?" And the answer is yes to both questions. To help him appreciate what he accomplished and interrupt his "would have, should have, could have" thinking, Alex filled out this postexposure chart.

Did I meet my realistic goal? How?	Yes. I walked up to Ginelle, smiled, and said hi.
Did I use safety behaviors? What did I do instead?	No. I spoke clearly and looked her straight in the eye.
How did I move toward my values?	I was friendly and I was true to myself.
What was the actual outcome?	She knows my name now. She knows that I am friendly and that I am interested in her.
What have I learned?	I said hi and it wasn't as bad as I thought it might be, and not as good as I had hoped, but okay and I am glad I did it.

Alex is in the pool now, up to about his ankles. This may seem like a small step, but it is an important one and it sure beats watching longingly from the deck. Ginelle may or may not remember him next time their paths cross, but if he continues using his compass he will get to know her better. He might become her friend, or he might find out that Ginelle really isn't his type and wind up pursuing other girls instead. Alex's world is opening up. It won't be perfect; he'll certainly make mistakes, and he'll probably have to tolerate lots of anxious thoughts and feelings, but it is a slightly bigger, more interesting world to live in now. Your world can be expanded too. Are you ready to act on what is important to you and move ahead toward your values?

At which end of the leash do you want to be?

On the next page are blank pre- and post-exposure forms for you. Remember to start with the least scary aspect of your avoidance situation, preferably one with a fear factor of less than 5. And remember that even though this is the lowest rung on your ladder, it should be treated as seriously as though it were the highest. Think carefully about each and every field in the charts. Each step helps you prepare for the next one.

Exposure	What feared situation are you facing?
Anxious Prediction	What are you afraid will happen?
Perfectionist Goal	How do you think you should act and appear in this situation?
Safety Behavior	What would you normally do to prevent your anxious prediction from happening?
Distortions	What distorted thinking does your anxious prediction rely on? ☐ **Catastrophic thinking** (assuming the worst possible outcome) ☐ **Discounting the positive** (refusing to take credit when you deserve it) ☐ **Labeling** (putting a negative name on yourself) ☐ **Spotlighting** (thinking everybody is watching you and/or how you feel inside shows on the outside) ☐ **Mind reading** (guessing what others are thinking or will think) ☐ **Social perfectionism** (setting a standard for yourself that doesn't allow for mistakes)
Coping Thought	What can you remind yourself of when you are feeling the most anxious?
Realistic Goal	What can you accomplish even though you feel anxious?
Values	What motivates you to move in this direction?

Exposure Date: _____ Time: _____

Did I meet my realistic goal? How?	
Did I use safety behaviors? What did I do instead?	
How did I move toward my values?	
What was the actual outcome?	
What have I learned?	

Chapter 10: Bella's Ladder
Exposure, Exposure, Exposure

Now that you've started doing exposures, you are on a new path, headed in an unfamiliar direction. You will need to consult your values compass often. There will be new, more challenging situations around every bend, and tempting avoidance detours that promise to quiet your fears. To continue forward and meet your goals, you will need to repeat the exposure process over and over. The good news is that every exposure, if done correctly, builds insight and confidence, making possible a life lived according to your values.

To help you understand how repeated exposures move you up the ladder, let's follow Bella as she climbs hers. Like you, Bella started off by choosing something from the master list of avoidance situations in chapter 1—in her case, situations where people would see her blushing. This avoidance has been a problem for her because it has gotten in the way of answering or asking questions in class, talking to her friends, and applying for jobs. And those things were all consistent with her values:

- to share more of herself and be known by others
- to go to college (she'd need to participate in class to get better grades)
- to be more independent

Bella made a list of the situations she'd have to stop avoiding in order to reach her goals. She started at the top with the scariest thing, and worked backward, listing less and less scary things toward the bottom.

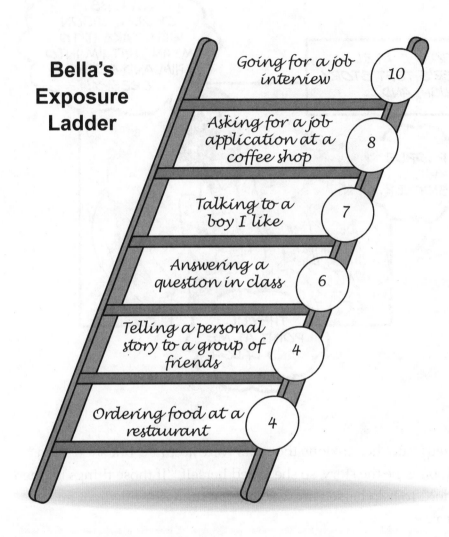

Bella's Exposure Ladder

Going for a job interview — 10

Asking for a job application at a coffee shop — 8

Talking to a boy I like — 7

Answering a question in class — 6

Telling a personal story to a group of friends — 4

Ordering food at a restaurant — 4

With no money for eating out, Bella decided to start out by telling a personal story to a group of her friends. Some funny things had happened when she went for her driver's test the previous weekend. The story would be easy to tell everyone in a text or online, but she had some very anxious thoughts about doing it face-to-face.

Bella was pretty sure her anxious thoughts were accurate, but she'd been dying to tell someone the story, so she asked herself, "If those things happen, what will I do?" To help herself answer that question, she filled out an exposure form.

Exposure	What feared situation are you facing? *Telling my friends a funny story face-to-face*
Anxious Prediction	What are you afraid will happen? *I'll blush really badly. Sammie and James will laugh and Jason will get creepy.*
Perfectionist Goal	How do you think you should act and appear in this situation? *Don't blush or show any signs of anxiety.*
Safety Behavior	What would you normally do to prevent your anxious prediction from happening? *Wear extra makeup. Cover my face.*
Distortions	What distorted thinking does your anxious prediction rely on? ☑ **Catastrophic thinking** (assuming the worst possible outcome) ☐ **Discounting the positive** (refusing to take credit when you deserve it) ☐ **Labeling** (putting a negative name on yourself) ☑ **Spotlighting** (thinking everybody is watching you and/or how you feel inside shows on the outside) ☑ **Mind reading** (guessing what others are thinking or will think) ☑ **Social perfectionism** (setting a standard for yourself that doesn't allow for mistakes)
Coping Thought	What can you remind yourself of when you are feeling the most anxious? *It won't last more than a minute before they start into something else. I can tough it out.*
Realistic Goal	What can you accomplish even though you feel anxious? *Telling the story without stopping or resorting to safety behaviors*
Values	What motivates you to move in this direction? *Sharing what I think about, being known to others*

After school on Friday, the topic of driving came up, so Bella swallowed hard, cleared her throat, and said, "You guys wanna hear about my driver's test?"

Bella was right about one thing. She definitely blushed. But her predictions of her friends' reactions were off. Here's what her postexposure chart looked like.

Did I meet my realistic goal? How?	Yes. I told the story.
Did I use safety behaviors? What did I do instead?	No. I wore just a little makeup and kept my hands away from my face.
How did I move toward my values?	I shared something personal and my friends all know me a little better.
What was the actual outcome?	I did blush and they did notice, but their reactions were friendly, not judgmental.
What have I learned?	My friends seem to accept the fact that I blush.

The next rung on the ladder was to test the danger of blushing in front of a bigger group by raising her hand and answering a question in class. Although she usually knew the answers, Bella never raised her hand; in fact, she sat in the back row and angled herself out of the teachers' lines of vision to avoid being called upon. She was certain that if she spoke in class everyone would look at her and notice her crimson face. Her last exposure had gone well, but it didn't give her enough courage for this. "After all," she thought, "they were my friends. I'm sure I won't get that kind of slack from my algebra class."

Bella's mind was reeling. Writing it all down in the chart really helped her organize her thoughts.

Exposure	What feared situation are you facing? *Raising my hand to answer a question in class*
Anxious Prediction	What are you afraid will happen? *I'll blush and the class will think I'm pathetic.*
Perfectionist Goal	How do you think you should act and appear in this situation? *Don't let them see that I'm scared.*
Safety Behavior	What would you normally do to prevent your anxious prediction from happening? *Wear extra makeup. Cover my face. Turn away from teacher!*
Distortions	What distorted thinking does your anxious prediction rely on? ☑ **Catastrophic thinking** (assuming the worst possible outcome) ☐ **Discounting the positive** (refusing to take credit when you deserve it) ☑ **Labeling** (putting a negative name on yourself) ☑ **Spotlighting** (thinking everybody is watching you and/or how you feel inside shows on the outside) ☑ **Mind reading** (guessing what others are thinking or will think) ☑ **Social perfectionism** (setting a standard for yourself that doesn't allow for mistakes)
Coping Thought	What can you remind yourself of when you are feeling the most anxious? *If kids are mean or judgmental to me, it says more about them than about me.*
Realistic Goal	What can you accomplish even though you feel anxious? *Answering the question*
Values	What motivates you to move in this direction? *Participating in my classes, preparing for college*

In math class the next day, just thinking about raising her hand brought a rush of blood to Bella's cheeks. She felt like she was doomed, but she rechecked her values compass and reminded herself where she wanted to go. When the teacher asked a question that nobody seemed to know the answer to, Bella inched her hand upward into the void.

It took several minutes for her heart to stop pounding and her cheeks to cool down, but Bella survived the test. She couldn't be sure, but it seemed as though her blushing didn't matter that much to the class. She filled out her chart as soon as she got home from school.

Did I meet my realistic goal? How?	Yes! I raised my hand and answered the question.
Did I use safety behaviors? What did I do instead?	No. I faced the teacher and did not cover my face with makeup or my hands.
How did I move toward my values?	I participated in class. That will help me get a better grade and help me get into college.
What was the actual outcome?	I blushed a LOT! But hardly anyone was even looking. The people who did look didn't react badly.
What have I learned?	I can sometimes get away with blushing in a big group.

It was halfway through May, and school would be letting out in a few weeks. Bella knew that if she didn't line up a job soon, she might be unemployed all summer. She decided to move up her ladder a couple of rungs and get a job application. Doing that was rated an 8, and Bella wasn't looking forward to it one bit.

But Bella didn't want to go back to her old avoidance behavior; she'd never get a job that way. To prepare herself, Bella took the time to fill out the following form.

Exposure	What feared situation are you facing? *Asking for application at a coffee shop*
Anxious Prediction	What are you afraid will happen? *I'll blush and the barista will think I'm uncool.*
Perfectionist Goal	How do you think you should act and appear in this situation? *Don't blush or show any signs of anxiety.*
Safety Behavior	What would you normally do to prevent your anxious prediction from happening? *Lower my head and pull up my collar.*
Distortions	What distorted thinking does your anxious prediction rely on? ☐ **Catastrophic thinking** (assuming the worst possible outcome) ☐ **Discounting the positive** (refusing to take credit when you deserve it) ☑ **Labeling** (putting a negative name on yourself) ☐ **Spotlighting** (thinking everybody is watching you and/or how you feel inside shows on the outside) ☑ **Mind reading** (guessing what others are thinking or will think) ☑ **Social perfectionism** (setting a standard for yourself that doesn't allow for mistakes)
Coping Thought	What can you remind yourself of when you are feeling the most anxious? *I can survive a few seconds of humiliation to move me closer to my goal.*
Realistic Goal	What can you accomplish even though you feel anxious? *Getting the application*
Values	What motivates you to move in this direction? *Being more independent*

Filling out the form really helped. It gave Bella just enough clarity and confidence to get her feet moving in the direction of the coffee shop.

Bella felt good. Getting the application without being humiliated was a surprise; none of her awful predictions had come true. "Even though I was blushing, the manager didn't notice," Bella thought. "Gotta love makeup!"

Oops!

There was something Bella had conveniently forgotten about. This time, she was wearing extra-heavy foundation to hide her blushing. If nobody could see her blushing, then she wasn't really exposed.

All shy people use sneaky or subtle avoidances that keep them from being completely exposed. Using tons of deodorant to hide sweating, mumbling to avoid being heard, not initiating conversation at a party, and drinking to lower inhibitions are all techniques for playing it safe. These safety behaviors trick us into thinking we are engaged in the world when we are actually avoiding it.

For Bella to keep climbing her ladder toward her goal of getting a job, she was going to have to repeat this exposure without using her safety behavior, without makeup. So she went to another branch of the coffee shop chain to ask for an application. This barista was a guy who looked right at her as the color rose in her face. Bella felt embarrassed, but he acted normal and told her the shop was a cool place to work. If Bella hadn't left right away, they might even have had a longer conversation. Bella felt relieved.

Here's the chart she filled out to evaluate her experience.

Did I meet my realistic goal? How?	Yes. I got the application.
Did I use safety behaviors? What did I do instead?	No. I did not wear heavy makeup and kept from covering up my face.
How did I move toward my values?	This is a step toward independence.
What was the actual outcome?	I did blush but he didn't seem to notice. And I got the application!
What have I learned?	Some people don't notice if I blush.

After she filled out the chart, Bella filled out her application. But as satisfying as it was to have her potential future job in hand, the thought of actually going in for an interview was terrifying. A solid 10!

"I just can't do it," Bella thought. She was dead certain of what would happen to her in a job interview. But Bella couldn't bear the thought of being unemployed and broke all summer. She decided that getting a shot at the long-term gain was worth some possible short-term pain. She and her friend Sandra got appointments to be interviewed at the coffee shop the same morning. Sandra dropped a bombshell at the last minute when she insisted that Bella comb her hair out of her face, saying, "So we can see you!"

"That's just my hairstyle," Bella insisted, but she realized that hiding behind her hair was a safety behavior, so before they left she added it to her chart.

Exposure	What feared situation are you facing? *Going for a job interview*
Anxious Prediction	What are you afraid will happen? *The manager will see me blushing and know I'm not fit to work behind the counter.*
Perfectionist Goal	How do you think you should act and appear in this situation? *Relaxed and confident*
Safety Behavior	What would you normally do to prevent your anxious prediction from happening? *Wear makeup, cover my face with my hair.*
Distortions	What distorted thinking does your anxious prediction rely on? ☑ **Catastrophic thinking** (assuming the worst possible outcome) ☐ **Discounting the positive** (refusing to take credit when you deserve it) ☐ **Labeling** (putting a negative name on yourself) ☐ **Spotlighting** (thinking everybody is watching you and/or how you feel inside shows on the outside) ☑ **Mind reading** (guessing what others are thinking or will think) ☑ **Social perfectionism** (setting a standard for yourself that doesn't allow for mistakes)
Coping Thought	What can you remind yourself of when you are feeling the most anxious? *The worst thing that can happen is that I won't get the job.*
Realistic Goal	What can you accomplish even though you feel anxious? *Going through with the interview*
Values	What motivates you to move in this direction? *Being more independent*

Going into the interview with her hair pulled back felt like the hardest thing Bella had ever done in her life. Here's the chart Bella filled out after the interview:

Did I meet my realistic goal? How?	*Yes. I made it through the interview.*
Did I use safety behaviors? What did I do instead?	*No. I let my face show the whole time!*
How did I move toward my values?	*I took a step toward independence.*
What was the actual outcome?	*I definitely blushed, but I made it through the interview. The manager seemed to like me.*
What have I learned?	*I am pretty sure she noticed my blushing, but she didn't seem to think it was a reason not to hire me.*

Bella didn't get that job, but she continued to go to interviews until she was hired. Funny thing Bella noticed about the ladder, though: the higher she climbed, the more rungs there seemed to be. Working a busy shift at a new job and dealing with people all day long rated 11 on her exposure ladder. Off the chart! But after what Bella had gone through, it was manageable. Her new experience has prompted some new, confident thoughts that speak almost as loudly as the anxious ones. Now she loves  following her compass and she is learning to accept herself, as well as the nickname her new boss gave her—Blushing Bella.

Chapter 11: **Troubleshooting**
What to Do When You Get Stuck

Exposures, like life, don't always go as planned. In this chapter we will explore the three most common problems that happen during exposures and how to deal with them.

1. **You planned an exposure and were psyched to do it, but when you got into the situation you felt much more anxious than you had predicted. Your impulse to avoid took over and you bailed. What to do?**

It is possible that you picked something too high on your ladder. If you think that is the case, pick a lower rung. If you do not have anything lower, brainstorm and see if you can come up with something.

For example, Liz, who thinks she is a boring conversationalist, planned to join a couple of friends at lunch and share two things she did over the weekend. She did join her friends but when the time came for her to talk, she got sweaty and started thinking it would sound weird to suddenly start talking about herself. Before the exposure, she had thought this would be pretty easy, and she did not have anything else on her ladder. To move it down a rung for next time, Liz came up with two ideas:

1. She could change the situation by choosing people she felt more comfortable with or talking with one person instead of two.

2. She could change what she was going to do by asking two questions, which was easier for her, and sharing just one thing she did over the weekend.

Liz decided to do the same exposure but with relatives who were coming over for dinner at her house.

Remember that it is perfectly normal to get anxious. In fact, if you are really anxious, you have picked something that you really need to work on. Conversely, if you aren't feeling anxious, you're ready for a higher rung. It is also normal that the more you do an exposure, the less anxious you will become and the more confidence you will gain, so at least you have that to look forward to.

Get a coach; sometimes involving a friend or even a parent can help you do your exposure. Just telling someone what you plan to do can help you stick to it. Depending on what your exposure is, you may be able to get someone to go with you when you do it. For example, when Bella went for a job interview, which she rated as a 10 in scariness, she took her friend Sandra with her.

2. **You are just as afraid doing an exposure for the tenth time as you were the first time you did it.**

Usually when you do repeated exposures you will experience a decrease, even if only a slight one, in your anxiety. When this doesn't happen, naturally it can be discouraging. But before you give up and go back to avoiding that situation again, take a look at what could be hanging you up.

Are you doing a safety behavior? You wouldn't necessarily be aware of it if you were, so take a hard look at how you have been approaching the exposures. Are you protecting yourself in some way from an embarrassing result? If you get through the situation without experiencing the actual risks, you will also miss the rewards. Remember, safety behaviors are like water wings. You are in the water, but you believe the only reason you are not drowning is that you're wearing them. Your fear of water isn't going to diminish until you actually have to paddle and kick to stay afloat.

When Bella went to the job interview wearing heavy makeup to hide her face, the makeup made it impossible for Bella to (a) test the probability that people would notice and/or comment on her blushing and (b) practice her ability to cope if they did notice and comment.

Doing exposures while maintaining your safety behaviors is like trying to learn how to ride a bike without ever taking off the training wheels.

Perhaps you are using disastrous distortions, those warped ways of thinking from chapter 4. Like a funhouse mirror, they are an inaccurate way of viewing yourself and the world.

Suspect number one is spotlighting. You may be so self-conscious, so aware of everything that you say or do that you have trouble getting into the swing of things. In a way, spotlighting is like another safety behavior. You are watching yourself super carefully so that you don't screw up.

Try taking the spotlight off yourself. Uncensor yourself; say what comes to mind. Pay attention to the people and the environment around you.

And while you are paying attention, make sure you are not negatively biased. Socially anxious teens tend to discount the positive things around them and overreact to the negative. Do you hyperfocus on any facial expression that might reflect boredom, disgust, disappointment, or irritation? It is common for anxious teens to misinterpret people's innocent facial expressions as being judgmental.

Is the situation you are practicing one you will always feel anxious in? In some cases, repeated exposure won't get rid of anxiety no matter how much you practice. Some activities are scary, but we do them anyway. As an extreme example, you might ride the roller coaster over and over, year after year, and yet your heart still pounds, you still scream, and you still hang on to the grab bar for dear life. Public speakers and stage performers still get butterflies in their stomachs before they step out in front of audiences, even after years of experience. We keep right on doing things that make us scared or nervous because of the rewards—the exhilaration of the G forces on the roller coaster or an audience's applause. Anxiety is an essential, normal part of the human experience. If you've done an exposure repeated times, anxious or not, you are now doing something you have avoided in the past.

3. **You do your exposure and things go wrong—horribly, terribly wrong!**

The most common thing that might make you think your exposure went wrong is when your anxious prediction comes true. Here are some examples:

- You blush and sweat, and someone comments on it by saying something like "Look at you blushing; how cute!"

- Your exposure is to start a conversation with someone. After you say hi, your mind really does go blank, and you stand there not saying anything more, just smiling, while the person walks away.

- You speak up in English class, giving an opinion on the book your class is reading, and another student rudely disagrees with you.

Are you using catastrophic thinking? Teens with social anxiety are hypersensitive to rejection and embarrassment. When something goes wrong, they tend to feel it really was catastrophic, that they are doomed to a life of ridicule and rejection. As we know from chapter 4, catastrophic thinking is a type of disastrous distortion that leads to more anxious feelings and more avoidance.
Trusting catastrophic thoughts to guide you is like letting your anxieties sit in the driver's seat.

If you suspect yourself of catastrophic thinking, ask yourself these challenge questions:

- *What did I do that was okay?*

- *What value am I moving toward?*

- *Am I 100 percent certain that my catastrophic thought is true?*

The fact is, learning to navigate bumps in the road will both help you become a better driver and get you where you want to go.

It's also possible that your bad result is actually good. The only truly wrong thing that could happen with your exposure is your not doing it. So if you did it, even if it did not turn out as you hoped, pat yourself on the back. Mission accomplished!

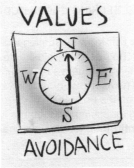

Regardless of the problem you may be having with your exposures—overwhelming fear, persistent anxiety, worst-case outcomes—the single most effective troubleshooting technique is to revisit your exposure chart. "What?" you may say. "I actually needed to fill those things out? Like a test or a school assignment?"

Skipping or skimming the charts is really tempting. Nobody enjoys paperwork. A lot of teens feel that they can wing it, that this stuff is so simple, that writing everything down is a waste of time. If you do exposures without a chart, you are more likely to go back to your old automatic thoughts and safety behaviors. And without taking the time to fill in the postexposure chart, you are more likely to obsess about not meeting a perfectionist goal and less likely to see the experience in a new way; that is, moving toward your values and doing what is important to you.

As an experiment, try charting the exposure you're having trouble with, starting with the first five sections, which are all about your fears and distortions. Take the time to think each question through, answering as honestly as you can.

Exposure	What feared situation are you facing?
Anxious Prediction	What are you afraid will happen?
Perfectionist Goal	How do you think you should act and appear in this situation?
Safety Behavior	What would you normally do to prevent your anxious prediction from happening?
Distortions	What distorted thinking does your anxious prediction rely on? ☐ **Catastrophic thinking** (assuming the worst possible outcome) ☐ **Discounting the positive** (refusing to take credit when you deserve it) ☐ **Labeling** (putting a negative name on yourself) ☐ **Spotlighting** (thinking everybody is watching you and/or how you feel inside shows on the outside) ☐ **Mind reading** (guessing what others are thinking or will think) ☐ **Social perfectionism** (setting a standard for yourself that doesn't allow for mistakes)

Those first five sections of the chart can be pretty tough to get through, but making an honest assessment of your unproductive thoughts, goals, and behaviors is a necessary step before you can come up with new ones. The next part of the chart is your cheerleading section. When the going gets tough, what can you tell yourself that will keep you from retreating? Remember to focus on what you can actually accomplish and why you are doing this in the first place.

Coping Thought	What can you remind yourself of when you are feeling the most anxious?
Realistic Goal	What can you accomplish even though you feel anxious?
Values	What motivates you to move in this direction?

Did you fill it out? Great! Review the chart as often as necessary. Share it with a trusted friend or an understanding parent. Exposures are like tests; better preparation tends to get better results. And once you've done an exposure, remember to fill out the postexposure evaluation. If you feel the exposure went badly, your answers to these questions will help you recover. If you feel the exposure went well, your answers will help set up the next rung on your ladder.

Did I meet my realistic goal? How?	
Did I use safety behaviors? What did I do instead?	
How did I move toward my values?	
What was the actual outcome?	
What have I learned?	

Managing your fears with charts and ladders can feel unnatural and tedious at first, especially before you begin enjoying the rewards your hard work will bring you. As you gain momentum and start getting closer to your goals, you'll start to understand your anxiety in a new way. Rather than fighting your fear, you'll learn to lean into it. What does it mean to "lean into the fear"? Read the next chapter to find out!

Chapter 12: **Above and Beyond**
How Mistakes Make You Stronger

In this chapter, we are going to encourage you to embarrass yourself. Maybe you'll ask a stupid question; maybe you'll bore someone. "On purpose?" you may think. "Are you kidding?"

It's not as crazy as it sounds. Remember, it was your attempts to prevent bad things from happening that got you on the avoidance path to nowhere. Doing your exposures so far, you have probably already suffered some embarrassment. And because you are still reading this book, clearly it has not killed you. In fact, you have probably discovered that you are stronger than you thought you were and that you've developed some coping skills. Now just imagine how powerful your coping skills could be if you exercised them purposely, actually making your anxious predictions come true.

Have you ever heard a skater say, "If you're not falling, you're not skating?" What that means is that real skaters are always challenging themselves beyond their ability, always trying new moves and bigger jumps. It's true that to get better in any sport we have to move out of our comfort zones, to lean into our fear and put ourselves at risk.

This is a lesson we learn during our first baby steps. Babies fall. They fall and they cry a lot. But what babies don't do is get embarrassed. Babies are not self-conscious about falling, even when everyone in the room is watching them. But let's just imagine a socially anxious baby girl who thinks that if she falls people will laugh at her, her parents will call her clumsy, or she will hurt herself and maybe even die. These thoughts would make her avoid trying to stand up and take those unsteady steps. She'd have to crawl everywhere she wanted to go, and that would be embarrassing too, so she'd wind up just sitting in place, playing it safe.

To learn to walk, you needed to learn to fall. To be comfortable in social situations, you must make embarrassing mistakes. You can wait for those mistakes to happen accidentally, or you can make them happen on purpose. Guess which method gets the best results?

Coming up with situations is easier than you may think. One thing you can do is go back over your anxious predictions forms, then think up ways that you can increase the likelihood of being embarrassed. There's your new exposure.

Here are some examples for Liz, Brandon, and Bella.

Liz thinks she is boring. She is afraid to draw attention to herself for fear that others will judge her. What does she do?

- She makes a list of boring topics and then talks and texts about them.
- She interrupts people on purpose.
- She yells across the hall to say hi to someone.

Brandon is worried he will say something wrong and make a fool of himself. What does he do?

- He orders something that he knows the restaurant doesn't serve.
- He calls someone by the wrong name on purpose.
- He mispronounces someone's name.

Bella is afraid people will notice she's blushing. What does she do?

- She rubs her cheeks hard before talking to people or making a presentation.
- She wears extra blush.
- She makes certain everyone notices her blushing, even if she has to point it out.

Here are some other above-and-beyond ideas:

- Spray water under your arms and on your forehead to mimic excessive sweat.
- Make your hands shake while you are drinking something.
- At the gym, count your reps out loud so everyone can hear.
- At your favorite clothing store, try on clothes inside out and ask the clerk how you look.
- At a convenience store, pay with a pocketful of change.
- When the teacher asks the class a question, raise your hand and answer it wrong.
- Call a pet store and ask if they sell dog food.
- Walk into a movie theater and sit in front of someone after the movie has started. Or set your phone alarm to go off an hour into the movie.
- Buy an ice cream cone, drop it, and ask for another one for free.

You get the idea. If the thought of it makes you feel anxious, chances are it would be a great exposure.

Conclusion

Understanding your social anxiety can help you realize that there are thousands of others exactly like you. Recognizing how distorted thoughts drive feelings and behaviors can help you question your thoughts and break the chain of avoidance. By facing fears one at a time, using coping strategies, and taking manageable risks, you can move from a life limited by social anxiety to one in which you can go where you want and have the friends you deserve.

If you have tried the techniques outlined in this book, hopefully you've experienced a decrease in your social anxiety and are able to do some things that you were avoiding before. To maintain the gains you have made, you will want to continue to practice your coping thoughts and pushing yourself to keep doing exposures. You are like an athlete in training; if you stop exercising, your muscles weaken. If you challenge yourself with regular workouts, you will get stronger.

There's no guarantee that your social anxiety will completely go away. Even after significant progress, you will undoubtedly still have days when you want to avoid situations that didn't bother you at all the day before. This is normal. Your level of anxiety, like other moods, can be influenced by lack of sleep, what you eat, menstrual cycle, and the use of alcohol and drugs, to mention just a few factors. If you can identify what seems to make you feel more anxious, you can help yourself by regulating that influence. In fact, just identifying it can bring some relief. For example, if you notice that you feel more anxious after a poor night's sleep, you can remind yourself that you will feel better when you are more rested.

Disruptive life events—like starting a new job, going to a new school or away to college, or moving to a new neighborhood or city—can all trigger an increase in social anxiety. These are all opportunities to review what you have learned in this book and practice the techniques.

So how can you tell whether you are really making progress? The best way is to look honestly at what situations you are avoiding. Your motto is Avoid Avoiding! If you are avoiding what is important to you, you have fallen into your old traps of social perfectionism or any of the other disastrous distortions. Get out your values compass, and remember what is important to you. Then turn to the skills that helped you before; they are the same skills that will help you again. Remember …

You are not alone

and

You can master social anxiety!

Appendix A: For Teens and Their Parents or Guardians About Therapy and Medication

This book is a self-help book. It explains what social anxiety is and how to get through it so that it does not get in the way of doing what you want in life. But sometimes self-help is not enough. If you are having trouble following through with the exercises and exposures in this book, or if you are doing the exercises but don't seem to be moving ahead, finding a therapist to work with may be what you need.

It is sort of like learning a sport. You might read about how the game is played and what you need to practice to get good at it, and yet still need a coach. Therapists are like coaches. They can work with you to develop the skills you need and point out things that you may not be aware of, like safety behaviors. They can also give you the encouragement to follow through with exposures that are especially challenging.

This book is based on cognitive behavioral therapy (CBT) and acceptance and commitment therapy (ACT). CBT focuses on the relationship between thoughts (cognitions), feelings, and action (behavior). A CBT therapist will help you identify and challenge the thoughts that are making you more anxious and change the behaviors that are making your problem worse. ACT is a type of CBT that focuses more on changing behavior and less on changing thoughts. The objective in ACT is to identify values and commit to actions that will lead you to live a more rich and meaningful life.

CBT and ACT are very effective for all anxiety problems, including social anxiety. If you decide to see a therapist, it is very important that you find one who is trained in CBT or ACT.

What to Ask a Therapist

You will want to feel comfortable with the therapist you see. You have every right to ask questions to make sure that the therapist you choose will be a good fit for you and has the experience to treat the issue you want to work on.

These questions are good ones for you and your parent or guardian to ask:

- What is your training in cognitive behavioral therapy? (Therapists will ideally be able to talk about workshops they have taken, experienced clinicians they have consulted with, organizations they belong to, and certificates they hold in CBT.)

- What is your training or background in treating social anxiety?

- How much of your current practice involves treating social anxiety?

- Do you feel you have been effective in treating social anxiety?

- What techniques do you use for social anxiety? (You want your therapist to talk about using exposure techniques and working with distorted thinking.)

If needed, are you willing to leave your office to do behavioral therapy? (Some of your exposures may require you and your therapist to be in public spaces.)

About Medication

You may be wondering or have heard about medication for social anxiety. In fact there are medications that can help with social anxiety, as well as other types of anxiety. There are basically two types:

Benzodiazepines

Benzodiazepines are relaxants that work very quickly in the body and brain. People usually take them when they become anxious or panicky or when they are going into situations that make them anxious.

Common benzodiazepines include Xanax (alprazolam), Valium (diazepam), Ativan (lorazepam), and Klonopin (clonazepam). Each name in parentheses is the generic version of the brand name and is based on the drug's chemical structure.

There are pros and cons to taking benzodiazepines.

Pros:

- They are quick acting.

- They can be taken as needed.

- They are not that expensive.

- Most people find it easy to take pills.

Cons:

- There can be side effects, like drowsiness, light-headedness, confusion, and depression.

- They can be deadly if you mix them with alcohol.

- They can become physically addicting.

- They can become a safety behavior that you are dependent on. Even if you are not physically addicted, they can get in the way of your facing your fears and gaining confidence in yourself.

Antidepressants

You may be wondering why antidepressants are prescribed for anxiety. The reason is that the way the drug works in your brain to decrease depression decreases anxiety as well. Also, it is not uncommon for people who have social anxiety to have depression too. These medications can help with both problems.

The most common type of antidepressants are called selective serotonin reuptake inhibitors, or SSRIs. Serotonin is a brain chemical that influences mood, and these drugs work by increasing serotonin levels; they also work on other chemicals in the brain that affect mood. Some common SSRIs include Prozac (fluoxetine), Paxil (paroxetine), Celexa (citalopram), Zoloft (sertraline), Lexapro (escitalopram), and Luvox (fluvoxamine). Other antidepressants that are sometimes used are Effexor (venlafaxine), Cymbalta (duloxetine), Serozone (nefazodone), and Remeron (mirtazapine).

Like benzodiazepines, SSRIs have pros and cons.

Pros:

- They are not that expensive.

- Most people find it easy to take pills.

- These medications are not addictive.

- Because you take these medications every day, as opposed to only when you feel anxious, they are less likely to be used as safety behaviors.

Cons:

- There can be side effects. The most common are nausea, diarrhea, constipation, drowsiness or jitteriness, dry mouth, headaches, yawning, shakiness, and sexual side effects, such as difficulty having an orgasm and/or decreased sexual drive. Many of these side effects decrease over time.

- These medications can take from four to six weeks to have a noticeable effect.

- Going off the medication can cause uncomfortable symptoms, like dizziness, nausea, headaches, difficulty sleeping, or flu-like symptoms. If you decrease your dose slowly when going off these medications, these effects will be less intense.

- When you stop taking these medications, social anxiety symptoms often come back.

Should you or shouldn't you take medication for your anxiety? Well, first of all, thinking you should or should not do anything is the wrong approach. These words imply that there is an absolute right and wrong for everyone, which is perfectionist thinking.

If you are experiencing extreme anxiety that is getting in the way of your functioning, like getting out of the house and going to school, or doing the exercises in this book, you may want to talk to your doctor about medication. It is usually a medical doctor who prescribes medication for anxiety, most commonly a family doctor, general practitioner, or psychiatrist (a medical doctor who specializes in mental health).

For those who try medication, the best results have been obtained by people who combine it with CBT. This makes sense. The medication can help lower the volume on your anxiety. The therapy will teach you skills to overcome the anxiety now and in the long run. That way, when you stop taking medication, you will be much less likely to experience a return of your social anxiety.

Helpful Resources

Books

My Anxious Mind: A Teen's Guide to Managing Anxiety and Panic by Michael A. Tompkins, PhD, and Katherine A. Martinez, PsyD

Freeing Your Child from Anxiety: Powerful, Practical Solutions to Overcome Your Child's Fears, Worries, and Phobias by Tamar Chansky, PhD

If Your Adolescent Has an Anxiety Disorder by Edna B. Foa, PhD, and Linda Wasmer Andrews

Websites

These sites offer information about anxiety, CBT, and ACT:

Anxiety Disorders Association of America: adaa.org/

This organization is dedicated to spreading awareness about the severity of anxiety disorders and effective treatments.

Association for Behavioral and Cognitive Therapies: abct.org

This organization focuses on promoting ongoing research regarding the effectiveness of therapies used to treat a variety of mental health conditions.

Academy of Cognitive Therapy (ACT): www.academyofct.org

This organization helps people access cognitive therapy resources, learn more about mental health disorders, and find a certified cognitive therapist.

Paruresis

If you have ever had trouble peeing in a public restroom, you are not alone. Most of us have experienced this at some time in our lives. The technical term for this problem is paruresis (pronounced par-yu-REE-sis). It is commonly referred to as shy bladder or bashful bladder, and it can range from mild to quite severe.

Millions of people suffer from paruresis, but they usually suffer alone because they are embarrassed to tell anyone. Shy bladder is caused by social anxiety. Sufferers are usually afraid of being watched, listened to, and in some way negatively judged. Their anxiety makes it impossible to allow urine to flow, no matter how full the bladder is. So not only is this problem embarrassing, it can also be very painful.

As we know, socially anxious teens will always attempt to avoid situations that make them anxious: in this case, peeing in a public facility, or even at home when there are other people around. This avoidance can really get in the way of living their lives and doing the things that are important to them. Going to restaurants, to friends' houses, to parties, or anywhere can be a big problem.

This self-test can help you figure out how much of a problem paruresis is for you.

Do you have a marked and persistent fear of using public restrooms while others are present? _____ Yes _____ No

Do you experience problems starting your urine in public facilities when others are present? _____ Yes _____ No

Do you worry about what other people are thinking when you are trying to urinate? _____ Yes _____ No

Are you able to urinate at home even though you can't do so away from home? _____ Yes _____ No

Are you concerned about being humiliated or embarrassed by problems passing urine? _____ Yes _____ No

Does attempting to urinate in public restrooms always, or almost always, make you anxious? _____ Yes _____ No

Does the fear of using public restrooms seem silly or unreasonable to you? _____ Yes _____ No

Do you avoid urinating in public restrooms and/or do you endure using public restrooms with intense anxiety and distress? _____ Yes _____ No

Does your avoidance of public restrooms, or anxiety and distress about using them, interfere significantly with your relationships, social activities, or work? _____ Yes _____ No

Has a doctor ruled out a physical cause for your difficulties urinating in public? _____ Yes _____ No

The more yes answers you gave, the more of a problem paruresis probably is for you. The good news is that the problem is very treatable with many of the same strategies outlined in this book. Because of the unique brain-bladder connection, however, there are specific ways to go about treating paruresis that are not covered here. These resources can help you learn more:

Shy Bladder Syndrome: Your Step-by-Step Guide to Overcoming Paruresis by Steven Soifer, MSW, PhD, George D. Zgourides, PsyD, Joseph Himle, MSW, PhD, and Nancy L. Pickering

Shy Bladder Center: shybladder.org

International Paruresis Association: paruresis.org

Other Common Types of Anxiety

People with social anxiety often have other types of anxiety as well. Here is a list of the most common types and some typical symptoms. While many of the exercises in this book can help with the problems listed below, it is best to learn about specific tools and exercises for each type of anxiety. The websites on page 118 may also be helpful for these types of anxiety.

Panic Attacks

- Suddenly feeling really scared when you don't expect it

- Physical sensations like racing heart, trouble catching your breath, or dizziness

- Fear of going crazy, dying, or losing control

- Fear of leaving your home

- Feeling trapped when in a store or in class

General Anxiety

- Worries that are hard to control

- Worry that you or someone you love might get hurt or die

- Worry about natural disasters like earthquakes, tsunamis, or hurricanes

- Worry about homework assignments, tests, or getting in trouble at school

- Worry about being late to things

- Physical symptoms like stomachaches and headaches

Phobias

- Fear of specific places like elevators, heights, or bodies of water

- Fear of certain animals or insects

- Fear of needles or blood

- Fear of vomiting

Obsessive-Compulsive Disorder

- Unwanted and unpleasant thoughts that get stuck in your head

- Fear of germs or getting dirty

- Worry that you hurt someone or did something bad

- Need for things to be even or just so

- Need to repeat certain actions even when you know it does not make sense

Separation Anxiety

- Fear of being along or sleeping alone

- Fear of being away from your parents

- Anxiety when you go to school, on field trips, or away overnight

Post-traumatic Stress Disorder

- Intense fear, helplessness, avoidance in response to a traumatic event

- Reexperiencing the trauma through flashbacks or nightmares

- Feeling numb and avoiding people, places, or activities that are reminders of the trauma

Jennifer Shannon, LMFT, is clinical director and cofounder of the Santa Rosa Center for Cognitive-Behavioral Therapy in Santa Rosa, CA. She is a diplomat of the Academy of Cognitive Therapy.

Illustrator Doug Shannon is a freelance cartoonist. He illustrated *The Two-Step*, a book that has been translated into several languages. He authored the nationally syndicated cartoon strip *Claire and Weber* from 1997 to 2000.

Foreword writer **Christine A. Padesky, PhD**, is a clinical psychologist and director of the Center for Cognitive Therapy in Huntington Beach, CA. She has more than thirty years of experience using cognitive behavioral therapy and is coauthor of *Mind Over Mood* and other books. www.mindovermood.com